Home-made Prayers

'Do you ever pray?'

A strange question for today – but Janet Green
was amazed at the response. Two-thirds of the
comprehensive school where she ????? admitted
to saying prayers fairly oft? ????? ??dn't
mind talking abou? ?

'In the firs? ????? ????ed, a second year told
me that he ??? ?ra???d yesterday. Yesterday being
Sunday, I as?ed if he went to church.

' "No," he said, "I went rabbiting."
' "What sort of prayers do you say when you go
      rabbiting?"
' "Please God let my ferret come out."

'We didn't reckon much to it as a prayer but it
raised interesting questions. What happens if the
ferret doesn't come out? And what if it does?
Next time that happens, he says he's going to
remember to say thank you.'

Illustrated by photographs taken by the teenagers
themselves, *Home-made Prayers* is a collection of
refreshingly honest conversations with God – some
more urgent than others!

Janet Green has written a number of books
for schools and worked on a television
series for the BBC. She is currently
Head of R.E. and Drama at Greenway Boys'
School in Bristol.

'Dear God,
I hope you don't mind home-made prayers.'

Home-made Prayers

Janet Green

A LION PAPERBACK

Published by
Lion Publishing
Icknield Way, Tring, Herts, England
ISBN 0 85848 211 0
Albatross Books
PO Box 320, Sutherland, NSW 2232, Australia
ISBN 0 86760 384 4

First edition 1983
Reprinted 1983

Acknowledgements
Cover photograph: Lion Publishing/Jon Willcocks
Text photographs: Greenway School/Ian Hayes,
Stephen Drew, Simon Potter, Michael Gazzard,
Ron Rogers
Special thanks to: Mark Packer, Ian Hayes, Syd
Senior, Paul Gilmore, Robert Welsman, Anthony
O'Reilly, Gary Brimble, Ricky Trimnell,
Tommy-Gun Figures, Neil Marsh, Mark Hopes,
Mark Cridge, Nicky Vowles, Iain Barron, Salman
Bhaidani, Neil Oxenham, Eddie Williams, Darren
Hawker, Julian Nelmes, Alan Sollars, Dean Hartley,
Alan Sharpe, Mark Gregory, David Hendy, Caroline
Woodley, Mortimer Boyce, David Soulsby, Tony
Ellaway, Stephen Hahn, Paul Sanki, Ken Gill,
Mollie Rose, Terry Ellans, Marcus Humphries, Alex
Flook, Rosemary Gerrish, Lee Green, Richard Jaap,
Melvin Coghlan, Gary Morgan, Michael Gamblin,
Ricky Trotham, Vicky Shaw, Brian Brown, Graham
Wilson, Raymond Beattie, the Colditz CB club and
P. Godfrey, Headmaster

Printed and bound in Great Britain by
Blantyre Printing and Binding Company Ltd,
Glasgow

Contents

Foreword

This book is a collection of prayers that boys in our school felt could be used by teenagers in the situations in which they find themselves. You may want to repeat our prayers but, most of all, we hope they will help you to work out your own.

Looking for teenagers to help with the book, I consulted all the classes in the comprehensive school where I teach. I was amazed at the response. Two-thirds of the school admit to saying prayers fairly often and didn't mind talking about it.

The material for these prayers was collected in the classrooms and if you study each prayer you will see the thoughts that had to be sorted out on each topic. In our investigations we learnt a lot about prayer but we learnt even more about people. Why is it that even non-believers get this urge to pray? Incidentally, the prayers at the end are on Christian topics but many of the earlier ones were worked on by teenagers of other faiths too. Some prayers are universal.

We felt sure that in this book we had to include some of those 'off-the-cuff' prayers that we collected on our way. You'll find them near the photographs. Those little 'home-made prayers' made us think. They'll have that effect on you.

Janet Green

'Ere Jesus

'Ere Jesus,
I've heard a lot about you, one way and another. It seems to me you lived a long time ago and some place a long way away – *I'm* not likely ever to go there. I don't know much about the whole scene. You dying for us and all that.
But I reckon, from what I've heard and what I've seen on the telly, that you knew where you were at, where you were going – and I reckon you knew what makes people tick. You never turned anybody away.
They tell me that you're still around and some people have eyeballed you and – well – I could do with a mate like you. God knows I've made a mess of it on my own.
I'd like to know where *I'm* at; and I'd like you to sort out where I'm going. I know it'll have to be a day-by-day thing. I guess there'll be a lot of changes. Give me the guts to face up to it. Help me not to care if folks think I'm some kind of nutter.
Give me a hand if the going gets rough and I'm tempted to pack it in. But with you in there with me I reckon I'll come out on top. And Lord, if I lose a few, put me straight.
Now Jesus, I don't know how YOU go about talking to people but, Lord, I want some copy from you.
Come in Jesus,
Breaker Break Out

First day at school

Dear God, I'm scared.
I've seen the big school.
We went last term to look round.
But you know what it's like, anyway.
There are big boys there.
We were the biggest in our school.
It's going to feel strange.
The teachers aren't like ours.
We'll be having lots of them.
We have to go to different rooms
        all round the school.
I'm frightened I'll get lost.
There's corridors all over the place, Lord.
I suppose you know all about that too.
Help me to find somebody to show me the ropes.
Please let me feel like I belong
        to this new school.
After all, it's my school now.

'Well, God, it's all over.
They didn't put my head down the bogs.
I think I'm going to like it. Thanks.'

Mogging off

Dear Jesus,
There wasn't any school in your days.
I wonder what you would have made of it?
You liked learning I bet.
Mind you, you seem to have known it all –
when you were twelve
you told those teachers a thing or two.
I could do with you giving me a hand.
In some countries they still pay to go to school
and people fought really hard to get the set-up
            we've got here –
so it must be a good idea.
Help me to see the point of it all.

'Dear God,
Don't let them find out
that I mogged off school.'

Bottom of the class

I came bottom again, Lord.
I feel a right dead loss.
I know somebody has to be bottom
but why does it always have to be me?
Sometimes I deserve it I suppose.
I could try harder.
But that will make it worse
if I come bottom again.
There's *something* I'm good at doing.
Help me to find it out.
Perhaps I shouldn't care so much
about coming last.
Help me just to enjoy the lessons
and learn as much as I can.
Amen

'Please God, could you let me
understand when Miss comes over.'

Wanting things

Dear God,
You must get really fed up of all the people
everywhere asking you for things. It wouldn't be so
bad if they were things worth asking for but mostly
it's just going on and on about things that don't
really matter. That's how it is if they're anything
like me.
I'm always asking for things, Lord. There must be
more to prayer than just asking for things.
I think the first prayers I ever said were about
wanting things. That's what most of my prayers
are about really. You know what I mean: let me
have a bike; let me do well; let me win; all that
sort of thing.
You've been good about it, Lord. You give me all
sorts of things, even when I don't deserve them
and when you know I'll forget to say thank you.
Mind you, I don't always get what I want. But
then I always think there must be a good reason
for you saying No.
I wonder why I bother to ask in the first place?
You know what I want before I begin.
You know better than me what I should be
asking for.
In fact, it would make more sense you doing the
talking not me.
   I'm not going to ask for anything tonight, Lord.
   I'll listen for a change.

Parents

Dear God,
They were young once.
Why can't they remember what it's like?
Perhaps they do remember.
Is that why they treat me this way?
It's for my own good, they say.
They know what's best.
Do they?
Even if they do, I'd rather find out for myself.
I wish I knew more about you
when you were young.
One day when you were twelve –
that's not enough.
But thanks for my parents anyway.
I suppose they try their best.
They're not really old.
I've seen them laughing
and behaving like kids.
Sometimes we're almost mates.
How can I meet them half way?
But there's one thing I'm sure of:
when I'm grown up I'll be different to my kids.
Won't I?

'Could you let our Ma win on the Bingo
'cos she hasn't won for a long time.
She was four away; then she was one away.
So could you let her win, please.
Thank you. Amen'

18

Fears

I get so frightened, Lord.
I worry about so many things.
What if something happens to my family?
Awful things happen to people sometimes.
Awful things could happen to me.
I don't want to think about the dark side of life;
but just a quick look
pulls me up sharp.
And maybe it's for the best.
I take so many things for granted, Lord.
So help me to be glad when I can.
I'm not going to close my eyes to my fears;
help me to face up to them.
Some of them are plain silly.
Help me to knock those on the head.
Some I can get over
with your help.
But some will turn out to be real.
I'll meet them head on when they come.
After all, you're there with me.
Please help all the people in the world
who live with fear and without you.

'Dear God,
Would you help my mum and dad to stop smoking
because they could die of cancer and have to
have a hole in their neck? I saw it on telly.'

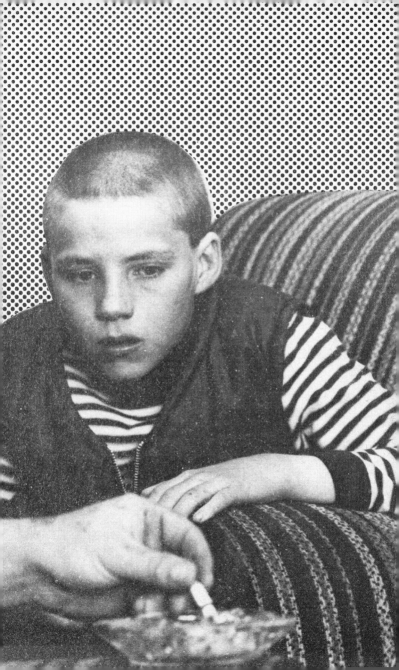

Getting lost

Dear God,
When I've got lost
I've sometimes said
help me find the way home.
It's not really a prayer –
but now I come to think about it –
perhaps it should be.
Help me never to get lost in life.
And thank you for sending Jesus
to show me the way home.
  In his name,
  Amen

A room of my own

Lord,
I haven't got a room of my own.
You know what that's like.
I get some stick from this lot.
So is it all right if I sort of mumble in my head?
I know you can hear me anywhere –
though it beats me how you manage to hear
          everybody at once.
But I suppose I shouldn't be scared of this lot.
OK Lord: hang on a minute
while I get down on my knees.

'Dear God,
Forgive my sins. Help those who are ill.
Let me go to Heaven –
I don't want to go just yet, mind.'

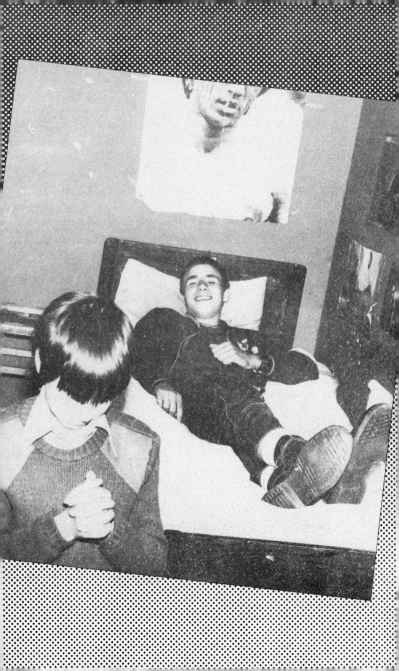

Totting up

Well that's another day over –
time for totting up.
First let me get rid of all the things
I should be sorry about.
Things I shouldn't have done.
And while I'm at it
the things I didn't know I shouldn't have done –
put me wise.
Some of these will get carried over
    into tomorrow, Lord.
That's the way things are.
Help me sort it out and make it right.
Help me to forgive myself
for those things I wish I hadn't done.
It's no use crying over spilt milk
so just let me learn by my mistakes
and know it's over and done with.
Just let me call it a day.
I am glad I had today.
There are some things I want to thank you for . . .
Now I've a few I want your advice on . . .
And some people who need my prayers.

Here goes . . .
Now about tomorrow,
I need to get ready for it.
Don't let me get out on the wrong side of the bed.
You know what I mean.
If I start off wrong
it goes like that all day.
A good night's sleep would help, Lord.
Now that's enough from me.
It's your turn now,
I'll keep quiet for a minute. . .

So now, Lord, thank you for today
and thanks in advance for tomorrow.
  In Jesus' name,
  Amen

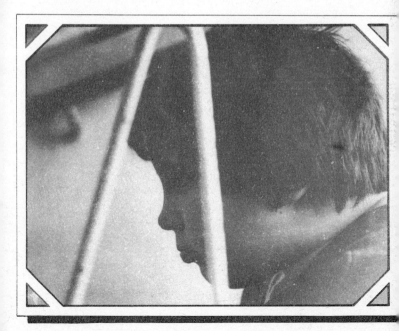

The gift of the gab

I could do with a gag sometimes, Lord.
I'm always opening my big mouth
and not thinking first.
I'm always chatting in class
and getting told off.
I answer back at home;
it just comes out, Lord.
I tell lies sometimes too.
Not just white lies
but whoppers.
And the trouble with lying
is that I don't seem to know when to stop.
I get carried away. Oh yes; and I exaggerate.
I swear too.
I can give a real mouthful
when I'm telling people to get knotted.
I'm sure you understand when something
        makes me blow my top
even though you wish I wouldn't.
But sometimes it's just plain habit.
I don't seem to have enough words.
And − OK I admit it −
sometimes I'm just trying to look big
in front of my mates.
It gives me the creeps to think you're listening too.
I wonder if you wish you hadn't invented talking?
It would have saved everybody a lot of trouble.
I don't really mean that, Lord. I just said it.
I suppose talking is like everything else −
it's there to be used
for good or bad.
So if I've nothing worth saying
help me to button my lip.

Pop idols

Dear Jesus,
Teacher says there are twentieth-century idols:
pop gods, film-star gods, money gods, car gods.
You name it, Lord, it's there.
I suppose I've got lots of gods
if you look at it like that.
Is it a good idea to have people to look up to, Lord?
When there's a lot of you supporting something
you feel you belong.
But really, if I want to be like anybody –
I'd rather be like you.
Amen

'I gotta thank you. It's only right innit?
After all what you done.
I think you're ace.'

Change

I just get used to something, Lord –
and everything changes. I change too. Every day.
That's growing up.
Sometimes I don't know whether I like it,
you get spots and things in your teens.
I get moody too.
The person I am inside, that seems to be different.
Please let those changes always be for the better.
But it's the changes around me I'm thinking about now.
The whole world moves so fast. School's not the same.
At home, too, things are different.
Help me to accept changes that have to happen;
to take them in my stride.
But it's not just the changes, Lord,
it's more than that. It's me.
You see, Lord, sometimes I get a say in the changes
        around me.
I keep having to make choices.
To decide things for myself.
I know it's only little things
but I suppose that it will happen more and more.
I'm not sure I like it.
Putting up with changes other people made
        was one thing.
This is another ball-game altogether.
Change is a funny thing, Lord.
I suppose it has to happen.
Sometimes people really struggle to get things changed.
But aren't there some things that shouldn't change?
How am I to know which is which?
Is that what wisdom is, Lord?
Please sort it all out for me.
Thank goodness you don't change.

Telegram prayers

So they call them telegram prayers.
That's news to me.
But I know all about them.
Those spur of the moment prayers.
I do them all the time.
A few quick words on the spot.
Like crossing my fingers:
It's a kind of superstition I suppose.
But I get the feeling
that you listen all the same.
They're OK for a standby,
these telegram prayers,
but I think it's time I said:
teach me to pray properly, Lord.
In Jesus' name,
Amen

'Please God let my ferret come out.'

Habits

Dear God,
About these habits I've got.
Help me to kick them.
Some are only little things,
like biting my nails.
But I don't want to be a slave to anything.
Help me to look after my body.
It seems stupid to neglect it.
It's one of the things I've got going for me
so why spoil it?
I don't want to be a fitness freak;
all I'm asking is
that you give me common sense
and the determination to follow it through.
Oh, by the way,
that goes for my head too.
The habits in my thinking.
Keep my mind clean;
don't let me waste my time on selfish daydreams.
Help me not to judge things
before I've looked at the evidence
and not to be biassed when I do.
It's so easy to be prejudiced about all sorts of things.
I know beliefs can't be proved, Lord,
that's what faith's all about;
but help me to know inside myself
what to believe.
I'm always asking your help, Lord,
that's becoming a habit.
It's one worth having, I suppose.
I pray that it will never become just an empty habit.
Shake me up if it does.

The Glue-Sniffer's Prayer

'Dear God,
I really wants to stop, God, but I can't.
I guess it's up to you to try and stop me.
It's getting on my nerves. When I eats my
dinner I spew, and when I go to bed I wet
the bed. And I thinks I better stop nicking
from the shop down the street. They're gonna
catch me. I used to nick from Woolworth's
but they don't sell it. I think I can feel my
brain rotting. I don't remember so good no
more. And stop my brother beating me up.'

Hand-me-downs

I had to make a list of my favourite things
and a list of those I don't like.
Teacher says I'm entitled to my opinions
like everybody else
but I wonder where I get them from?
I must have got them from somewhere.
I hate having to wear hand-me-down clothes
so I sure don't want second-hand ideas.
What I believe —
that's one thing
that's got to be all mine.

The CB Prayer

Our Big Daddy on the clouds
everywhere's your twenty.
Give me a copy.
You're wall to wall and tree top tall,
really you're above giving any handle to.
Give us this day our green shields and nose-bags
and everything else we need.
Forgive us our wind-ups
as we forgive dipsticks and wallys;
help us to stay clean and green
and save us from all kinds of Buzbies.
I want to put myself on your channel
to bring in a world where everybody's good buddies,
where lingo is meant for linking up
not breaking up
and where nobody goes ten one.
Roger Dodge; in the Superstar's name
all the wondidundis are yours on all channels,
ten ten till we do it again,
breaker break.

P.S.
You don't need a rig
to talk to Mister Big!

Being bullied

Dear God,
I don't know what to do.
There are some big boys and they said,
'Give us some sweets and we'll take care of you.'
It doesn't seem right to me.
It isn't right, is it?
It's funny how you start a prayer and then
you know the answer when you're half-way through.
So, God, if they ask me for money tomorrow,
give me the strength to say
'Get lost'.
Amen

In the soup

Oh God,
I've left it a bit late.
Only asking for help now I'm in trouble.
It seems a bit tight, I know.
I just didn't think about it before.
I'm really sorry.
To be fair, maybe I wouldn't have been sorry
if I hadn't been caught.
So maybe it's for the best.
But now I really am sorry.
Help me to be sorry for the right reasons.
With your help I'll show that I'm sorry.
With your help I'll never do it again.
I'll try and make up for it, Lord.
Only, where do I go from here?

The lesser evil

Dear God,
I don't know which way to turn –
whatever I do will be wrong –
whatever I do, somebody will be hurt.
I know it's my own fault –
I should never have got in this mess
in the first place.
Help me to choose the lesser evil
and by your grace
turn it to good.
  In Jesus' name,
  Amen

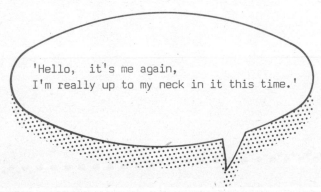

Revenge

Dear Jesus,
You forgave everybody.
Help me not to keep wanting
to get my own back.
Help me not to bear grudges.
Help me not to be glad when things
        go wrong for people I don't like.
Don't let me always want to have the last word.
You know what I'm like. I take the huff so easily.
Help me to stop before things get out of hand.
It only starts with something stupid in class
and next minute we're at the gate at home time
set up for a fight.
Help me to admit when it's my own fault
and not to shift the blame.
Help me to try and see other people's
        points of view.
I suppose what I really want to say is:
help me to love other people. No matter what.
After all, Jesus, that's the way you love me.

'I went too far today, Lord. I got my own back. But I wish I hadn't done it.'

Loving others

Dear Jesus,
About loving other people.
I find it hard enough to like some of them.
If we did love everybody
I suppose there wouldn't be any murders
or any wars.
Nobody would steal from anybody else either,
they'd stop and think
how the other person might feel.
It's the answer to everything
isn't it?
But how do I start?

'Dear Jesus,
Two boys in our class went to a campaign.
They asked our teacher about being saved.
She wants to send them to our church.
They'll ruin everything.
Can't you find somewhere else to send them?'

Job's prayer

Sometimes, God,
I can't forgive you
for the things you let happen.
I know that's a terrible thing to say.
But I want to be straight with you.
I know you do
fantastic things for people
but it's when you don't
that worries me.
I kick about it all the time.
I try to count the good things
but it feels like I'm conning myself.
It happened, Lord.
There's nothing good can come from it.
Is there?

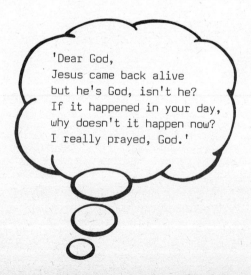

Rainy days

Dear God,
Why do people pray for good weather?
I've often wondered about it.
Do you change the weather?
It must get awful complicated if you do.
It's all very well wanting sunshine for trips' day
but the farmers might not be so pleased about it.
They like a spot of rain.
I suppose you've a big enough job
just keeping things going.
That's a miracle enough when you come
    to think of it.
But all of it puzzles me, Lord.
Not just miracles but all the rest of that
    supernatural stuff.
I can't see that anything can count as more
    than natural.
Is it just a way of saying
that it's more than we can understand?
To YOU it wouldn't seem supernatural.
So why am I praying for good weather?
It's not the weather that needs changing –
it's me.

'Dear God,
It's raining again today.
Help me to keep cheerful even when the weather
is miserable.'

Putting on the style

Dear Lord,
I wish I didn't care so much what I look like
 to other people.
I'm always wondering what they think about me.
Especially now. Now that I've met her.
I want her to like me, Lord.
But there's something that's worrying me.
You see, Lord, it's all pretend.
There's this gear, the hair, the way I go about things,
but inside it all somewhere, there's me.
It's like the way I used to muck about
just to be like my mates.
That wasn't me, either. It's all a front, Lord.
Is everybody like this? I suppose they are.
Does it get easier when you get older?
Do people ever stop pretending?
But I can't pretend with you, Lord.
You know me better than I do.
Even when I'm trying to follow you
I sometimes wonder if I'm just putting it on.
I'd like to think I'll grow to be like you if I keep on.
With your help of course.
I've just had a thought Lord — is she pretending too?
I don't want us to have to pretend to each other.
I don't think I've ever looked further than
 the image she's got.
She's ever so pretty, Lord.
Help me to learn to see the real people there
 inside everybody.
Not to judge by clothes and badges
and things that don't matter.
And, Lord, don't let me forget about this tomorrow.
I'm seeing her after school.
And — well, I told you, Lord, — she's ever so pretty.
And I think she fancies me.

'Help me to stay cool and play hard to get.'

Jilted

Dear God,
He doesn't love me.
I feel such a fool, Lord. Is it just my pride that's
hurt? But it's awful when somebody doesn't want you.
I pleaded with him, Lord. I knew there was no
point even when I was doing it. I know you can't
force somebody to love you.
I promised to change, to be anything he wanted.
But it was no use. I know it was silly saying all
those things. If I did get him back I think I'd be
the loser.
But I don't want to live without him. I can't
understand why he's gone off me.
I know that I should be glad that YOU love me
and that's the thing that matters. But, honestly, I
admit it's just not the same. I want him so much.
Even if he's not right for me.
I was going to ask you to get him back for me, Lord.
But that's not it, is it? That's not the prayer.
OK Lord, you win. Just help me not to go on
making a fool of myself. I do love him, Lord, so I
suppose that's another reason to let him go. Help
me not to feel the way I do every time I see him.
And stop that sick feeling I get when he's with
somebody else.
Don't tell me there's more fish in the sea. Don't
tell me I'll get over it. Just get me through, day by
day.
And Lord, help me never to hurt anybody the way
he's hurt me.
   In Jesus' name,
   Amen

'Dear God my life is in ruins.
Is it wrong to like him so much?'

Food

I wouldn't like to live on a handful of rice a day.
Some people do –
and that's if they're lucky.
I get worried about them.
It doesn't seem fair.
What can we do to help?
Thank you for the things I eat.
Give me the sense not to fill myself
with junk food.
Help me to be willing to try something new
and not turn up my nose at it.
Help me not to have eyes bigger than my belly.
Not to waste food.
I think I take it too much for granted.
Thank you for the people who grow food
and for the people who get it ready.
I suppose if I really mean this
I ought to help with the washing-up.
While I'm doing it
I'll think of all the other things
there are to thank you for.

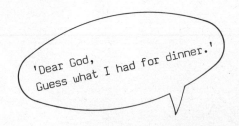

When plans go wrong

Dear God,
It's so hard sometimes
when I don't get something
and I was sure it was for me.
It doesn't seem to make sense –
not from where I stand.
There must be a plan behind things that happen
and not just for the big things in history.
Either the whole lot's planned
or none of it.
So if there's a plan for me
how do I go about fitting in with it?
And if I went wrong
would that be part of the plan too?
It's no wonder people sit back
and say it's all fate.
But you can't have meant us to do that.
Is there something else waiting ahead for me?
Was this one just to keep things ticking over
till the time was right?
Help me to see the pattern in things that happen.
I'm sure you've got it all mapped out.
   In Jesus' name,
   Amen

'Dear God,
I didn't get the job.'

Peace

It doesn't seem fair, Lord.
Don't they realize that we carry the can
        for what they do?
They're so old.
They won't be alive to see it through
and we'll have to sort it out.
The world's changing so fast, Lord.
It turns me cold to think that they don't know
        the answers.

What chance have *we* got?
They even fight about religion, Lord –
or that's the excuse they make.
I think they just like fighting.
I know we have to fight for things we believe in.
But God, I like living. I don't want a nuclear war.
You can't have meant that to happen.
So it's one prayer where I know
I'm on safe ground.
I suppose the things that we decide
when I'm grown up
will be left for the next lot to sort out.
I hope we make a better job of it.
So give us peace Lord.
Show us where to start. Here. Now.
In me.

'Dear God,
I'm frightened they'll blow the world up.'

Christmas

Dear Jesus,
They say we've lost the message of Christmas.
I know what they mean.
It's all buying and selling
and wondering what you're going to get.
Everybody eats too much –
I know I do.
But does it really upset you
the way they keep it?
At least they remember once a year
even if they don't get the point.

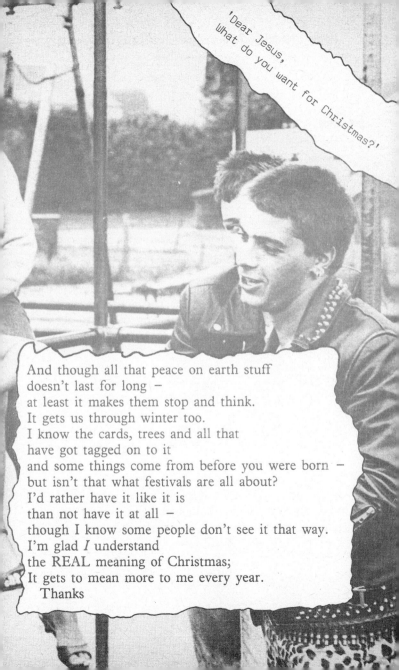

'Dear Jesus,
What do you want for Christmas?!'

And though all that peace on earth stuff
doesn't last for long –
at least it makes them stop and think.
It gets us through winter too.
I know the cards, trees and all that
have got tagged on to it
and some things come from before you were born –
but isn't that what festivals are all about?
I'd rather have it like it is
than not have it at all –
though I know some people don't see it that way.
I'm glad *I* understand
the REAL meaning of Christmas;
It gets to mean more to me every year.
    Thanks

Ash Wednesday (The beginning of Lent)

Dear Jesus,
I'm a follower of yours so I'd like to keep Lent
this year. There wouldn't be much point otherwise.
I've been thinking about that time you spent in the
wilderness. You'd just been baptized and you were
working out what you were going to do. Being the
Messiah and all that.
I bet some of the ideas were hard to kick. You
could have fed everybody who was starving. You
could have proved who you were. That would have
been easy enough. I bet you felt like proving it to
yourself sometimes, too. You could have gone into
politics and ruled the whole world. Your mates
wanted you to do that.
I'm glad you didn't give in. You kept it up right
through, even when they challenged you to get off
the cross and you wouldn't. I'm glad for our sakes
that you said No.
You didn't give in and you can help me not to give
in. Not just my promises for Lent but always.
I don't know what the Devil looked like when he
tempted you. Help me to recognize him even when
he isn't in all his gear; when he's just a nagging
voice in my head. I wish I knew the Scriptures the
way you did. I'm working on it.
I know Lent is not only about giving things up.
Help me to put more effort into everything I do as
well; right through till Easter. I reckon if I can
manage forty days with your help then the same
goes for the rest of my life.
Amen

'Dear God,
I'm giving up sweets again this year.
Hope that's all right with you.'
£4.10
90
£1.35
£1.70
£2.52
£1.60
£1.78
SWEET PEANUTS
TURKISH DELIGHT
MURRAYMINTS
AMERICAN HARD GUMS
NUT TOFFEE
CHOCOLATE BRAZILS
VANILLA FUDGE
BARLEY SUGAR
CHOCOLATE PEANUTS
SUGARED

Palm Sunday

Dear Jesus,
I wonder what I would have made of it all
if I'd have lived then?
I hope I wouldn't have thought you were mad.
Some people did –
even in your own family.
Would I have thought you were bad –
some sort of con-man –
out for what you could get?
Or would I have believed
that you really are the Messiah?
And if I did
would I have ever let you down?
It's awful to think that some of those people
      crying, 'Hosanna'
were shouting 'Crucify him!' only a week later;
and it so easily
might have been me.

From a home-made poem:

'He didn't come
In a war chariot
So he was betrayed
By Judas Iscariot.'

Thoughts on Good Friday

Dear Jesus,
I suppose everybody should have expected
    you'd have to die.
That's what usually happens to people
who talk sense and nobody wants to listen.
They don't like people to be different.
But there was more to it than that.
It was some sort of plan.
I find it all very puzzling.
If you were a ransom, Lord,
who were you paying it to?
It wasn't being paid to the devil, was it?
Was it to God?
I didn't think God was like that.
But I suppose he has to keep the rules, too,
even if he made them.
It showed how much you loved us though
and that's what really matters.
And I like the bit where you forgave everybody.
I learnt a big word today:
atonement.
The preacher reckons you made us
at one with God.
I'm catching on, I think;
maybe you'll help me understand.
But anyway, Jesus,
there's one thing I know:
you died for me.
Thanks

Thoughts on the Resurrection

Who *did* move that stone?
I'd love to have been there.
All sorts of people saw you,
even that brother of yours – James.
I didn't reckon much to him.
But then the Bible is
full of people you couldn't call heroes.
They made the same mistakes as we do –
they were just like us.
You made a difference to them
the way you do to us.
I think I'd be a Christian
even if there was no heaven or hell;
It means so much
just having you here day by day.

'I did my first witness today, Lord,
just like you said.
I told them I'm born again.
They thought I meant reincarnated -
That might have gone down a bit better.
They thought I was having them on, Lord.
Even the teachers don't believe I can change.
I'd better try again tomorrow;
Wish me luck.
Amen'

Struggling with the Holy Spirit

This Holy Spirit thing –
it baffles me.
I can understand about God –
You've only to look at the things he made;
so that's all right.
As for Jesus –
well, I feel I know him;
But this Holy Spirit
is beyond me.
Calling him the Holy Ghost
only makes things worse.
I wonder why there had to be the three of them:
God, Jesus and the Holy Spirit.
It must be an important subject –
people fought about it –
churches split over it.
I don't reckon any words
could ever get it spot on right.
Is he like my conscience?
And this Power that people can get –
is it like electricity?
Well as long as it works
I don't suppose it matters
that I don't understand it all.
It beats me, this Holy Spirit.
I don't like to feel I'm leaving him out;
but who is he?

The Second Coming

Dear Lord,
What's this about you coming back again?
It's a bit scary –
you could turn up any minute;
I'd better watch my step.
Will it be on TV?
I wonder why you didn't come like that
     in the first place?
I suppose it wouldn't have given us a chance;
there wouldn't have been any doubt about it –
that you were
who you said.
But there'll be no doubt about it next time –
so help me make sure I'm ready.

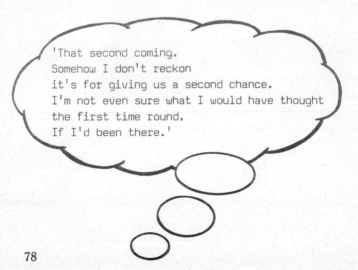

'That second coming.
Somehow I don't reckon
it's for giving us a second chance.
I'm not even sure what I would have thought
the first time round.
If I'd been there.'

P.S.

'Dear God.
Thank you for making the world.
I've prayed all week
ever since Miss told us about prayers.
What happens now?'